Guitar

Music Book for Beginners

Guide-How To Play Guitar Within 24 Hours, Easy And Quick Memorize Fretboard, Learn The Notes, Simple Chords

by

Tom Mahalo

Tom Mahalo

written permission from the publisher. All rights reserved.

The information provided herein is stated to be truthful and consistent, in that any liability, in terms of inattention or otherwise, by any usage or abuse of any policies, processes, or directions contained within is the solitary and utter responsibility of the recipient reader. Under no circumstances will any legal responsibility or blame be held against the publisher for any reparation, damages, or monetary loss due to the information herein, either directly or indirectly. Respective authors own all copyrights not held by the publisher.

The information herein is offered for informational purposes solely and is universal as so. The presentation of the information is without the contract or any type of guarantee assurance.

Tom Mahalo

Tom Mahalo

Contents

Introduction

I want to thank you and congratulate you for purchasing the book, *"Guitar - Music Book for Beginners* Guide- How to Play Guitar Within 24 Hours, Easy and Quickly Memorize Fretboard, Learn the Notes, Simple Chords."

This book can help you learn the guitar in record time. Make sure you keep focused on training and use all your knowledge you already have about music. Keep in mind that everyone is different, playing guitar is all about practicing, training and getting better and better every time you hold your guitar. I did my best to make this book as easy as possible so everyone could play some of the bonus songs in a really short period of time. I believe in you! You can do it! Trust in yourself! Don´t wait and practice, practice, practice! Good luck!

If you would love to learn how to play the guitar but have not had the courage to pick it up or tried playing a chord because the scores of notes and the complex fretboard (finger board) has been scaring you, you have landed at the perfect spot.

This book is the complete, how-to-play guitar guide for newbie guitar players. If you want to develop guitar playing skills and want to become a maestro guitar player one day, this book is precisely the help you need right now.

Start reading and implementing the steps discussed in it and you will most certainly be able to play your guitar by the end of the day. Sounds exciting, right? If your answer is in the affirmative, what are you waiting for?

Thanks again for purchasing this book, I hope you will enjoy reading it!

Lesson 1: The Fundamentals

If this is your first time playing the guitar, or at the very least, your first time learning how to, it is extremely important to learn guitar playing fundamentals before we move on. That is the sole aim of this section: to teach you the fundamentals.

Basic Guitar Parts

Whether you are planning to play an acoustic or an electric guitar, you will eventually be dealing with metal and wood. You will be holding a wooden structure that will resonate the sound produced by the copper-wound strings. This will create the beautiful, soothing, and warm tones associated with guitar playing. Therefore, it is essential you know the basic guitar parts before setting your hand on it.

The guitar strings run between the guitar's headstock, which is the pentagonal shaped structure at the top of a guitar. The strings affix to the tuning pegs, which you can rotate to tighten as well as slacken the strings.

The bridge is the point where these strings affix to your guitar's body. The strings on an acoustic guitar affix to the bridge using removable pegs, whereas those on electric guitars are strung through the eyelet.

The neck refers to the long piece of wood on the guitar that is flat on the front side and curved on the backside. The flat front is the fretboard; it contains the metal frets demarcating the different guitar notes. Acoustic guitars contain a sound hole in the guitar body where the sound resonates,

whereas electric guitars contain around two to three magnetic pickups that channel the guitar's sound to an amplifier.

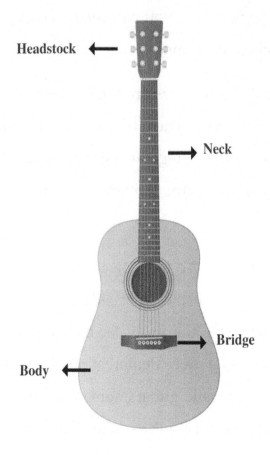

Holding The Guitar

If you are right handed, you will play your guitar by strumming almost halfway between your guitar's bridge and its sound hole using your right hand and will be fretting the guitar strings on its neck using the left hand. If you are left handed, you will strum its strings with your left hand and fret the strings with your right one.

To play the guitar, sit straight in a comfortable, straight-backed stool or chair. While orienting your guitar towards your body, make sure that its smallest string points towards the floor and its thickest string points upwards at the ceiling. Hold its back so it softly touches your tummy as well as chest and is resting on the leg of your respective strumming hand.

Your leg will do the job of holding up your guitar. You will cradle it to the rest of your body. Your left hand will stabilize its neck and fret the strings if you are right handed. Hold its neck in the 'V' shape created by the forefinger and thumb of your right hand. If you hold the guitar in this manner, you will be able to move the left hand upwards and downwards very smoothly down the guitar's neck and will not need to hold it.

Try not to hunch your back.

Guitar angled TOWARDS you slightly

Dip of the guitar resting on the lap the same side as strumming hand

Even if you follow these guidelines and hold your guitar perfectly, you are going to experience a little discomfort at the start. This is perfectly normal since you are not used to holding and strumming your guitar. Please do not feel discouraged if you feel a pain in your shoulder, hands, neck, and arms. You are going to get used to it in a couple of days. Be strong and keep going. ☺

<u>Lesson 2: Tuning Your Guitar</u>

After going through the basics and learning to hold your guitar like a pro, you need to tune it. No fun comes from playing an out of tune guitar. When you play/practice guitar with an out of tune guitar, it will lead to poor guitar playing habits. Regular tuning will familiarize you with the different guitar strings as well as the notes produced by different fret combinations.

There are lots different tuners you can choose from. One of many is a digital clip-on tuner. Is incredibly easy-to-use and extremely accurate. You can get it for $10 – 25.

Note: if you have a calibration setting on your tuner. Set your tuner to A 440 Hz. This is for the standard tuning frequency.

This is going to work for your acoustic guitar, electric guitar, nylon string guitar as long as it's not a baritone guitar.

The first thing you are going to need to now are the notes that the strings are actually tined to. So the notes are going to be: E, A, D, G, B, E.

The way that this tuner works is that there is a needle, and if it's straight in the middle, then you know that your string is in tune. If it's over to the left, then you know that you are a little "flat". If it's to the right, then you know that you are too far above the note, or what we call "sharp".

So let's practice and play this first string E and see where you land. So if you can see when you are a little bit to the left, which means we are "flat". You'll go ahead and tighten this string up by turning it counterclockwise until the tuner turns green and we know that we are in tune.

If you can see that you are below the note then again, turn machine head counterclockwise until tuner turns green, and you are in the middle.

Proceed this same steps with all the rest strings A, D, G, B, E. Beautiful, now the tuner's telling us that we are in tune and ready to play.

Learning The String Names

The Open strings

First, you must learn the names of all the strings. It's a very important thing to know the note names of the open strings on your guitar. You need to know this when you buy a replacement string for your guitar (e.g., "can I please have a D string") and it will help you learn the names of the notes that you are playing. Knowing the names of the strings will also help you use a guitar tuner, memorize the chords and it is really important to know the names of the string before you start to play anything on the guitar. From the thickest to the thinnest string, all the strings have names. The thickest string is E and produces the lowest pitch, while the thinnest string is also E and produces the highest pitch. The other strings in between are A, D, G and B. You can remember the string names with the help of this mnemonic,

'**Eddie Ate Dynamite, Good Bye Eddie!**'

1st string - **E** (the thinnest)

2nd string - **B**

3rd string - **G**

4th string - **D**

5th string - **A**

6th string - **E** (the thickest)

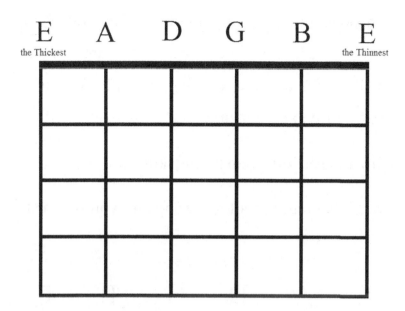

One of the best ways to remember is to make up rhymes, here are some examples you can use or make up your own rhymes.

From Thin to Thick

Easter **B**unny **G**ets **D**runk **A**fter **E**aster

or

From Thick to Thin

Eddy **A**te **D**ynamite, **G**ood **B**ye **E**ddy

Tom Mahalo

The open strings are the starting point for all the notes on each individual string. Make sure you play on those for a while, one by one, all together so you get use to their sound.

How to read the Chord diagram

Chord diagram has all six strings on your guitar E, A, D, G, B, E.

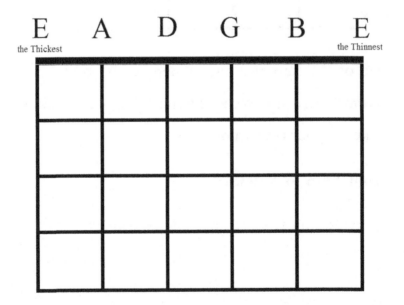

E A D G B E

the Thickest   the Thinnest

And also shows the frets, you can see them as the "rows" and there is the little metal stripe that runs across the neck of the guitar and that divides the neck of the guitar to many frets. On each Diagram, you see frets as rows.

	E	A	D	G	B	E	
							Nut
1st Fret							
							metal stripe
2nd Fret							
							metal stripe
3rd Fret							
							metal stripe
4th Fret							
							metal stripe

You can also see the bunch of the X's and o's there on the top of Chord diagrams. So whenever you see X there, it means that you are not going to play that string.

For example **chord A** you see the X for the thickest string E, that means you will only play strings A, D, G, B, E- the thinnest. We also see a lot of little circles o's which means that you will play that string but there will be no finger on it, you just play an open string there. The big circles show where you need to put your fingers on, what fret and what string to play the chord correctly.

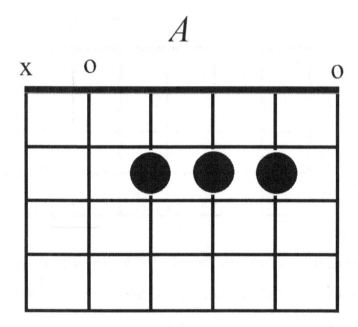

What about the next **chord D**? Would you be able to find out what strings to play, and where to put your fingers to play this D chord correctly? I am sure you will, so let's do this.

D

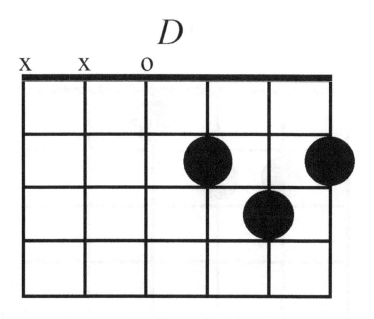

Okay, perfect let's just make sure we got it right. For chord D we will only play strings D, G, B, E, and D string will be open with no finger on it.

Now let's move to the next one which is **chord E**. What strings will we play? Can you tell?

E

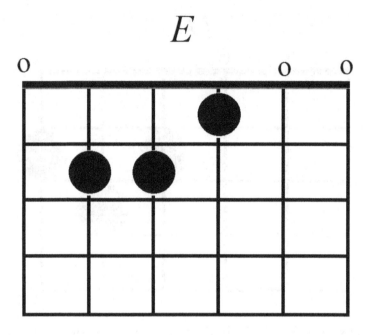

For this chord E, we will play all the strings, that is correct. We will play open strings E, B and E and for A, D, G we will place fingers on those.

Fretting Guitar Strings

Next, practice fretting your guitar strings. Frets are the thin metallic stripes running perpendicular to your guitar's strings marking every note. To play a note, gently press your finger downwards between two metal strips while making sure not to press on them.

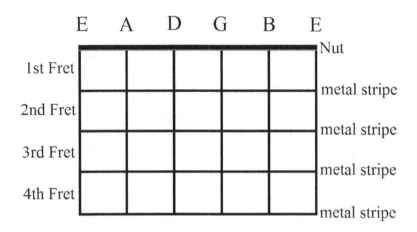

For instance, if you are playing the third fret, your finger will be lying on the string positioned in the gap right between the guitar's second and the third fret. Additionally, ensure your finger sits close to the lower fret to avoid buzzing.

Hold down the string very firmly so it vibrates only between the hand strumming the string and the finger holding it. Each time you move your finger from one fret to the second one, the pitch resulting from the movement will be ½ step higher if you move towards the guitar's body and will be ½ step lower if you move towards the guitar's headstock.

Practice moving downwards and upwards on the fretboard as well as pressing the frets to familiarize yourself with fretting. Moreover, concentrate on memorizing the fretboard (we shall thoroughly discuss how to do this in the next chapter).

Holding The Guitar Pick

A plectrum or a pick is a tiny tear-shaped piece made of plastic and is used to pick out the individual notes on the guitar and strum them. Picks are extremely cheap and are easily available at music retailers. While it is not essential to play a guitar using a pick, it is ideal to learn how to use one.

To use a pick, form a fist using the hand you will use to hold the pick. Keep your thumb perfectly flat on top of your four curled fingers. Now, hold your pick by placing it perpendicular to the fist you formed using your index finger and thumb. Make sure only a couple of centimeters of the pick's smallest end stick out of your hand. The image below illustrates this description well.

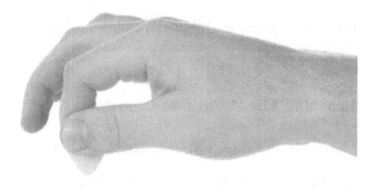

Practice holding it a few times and you will surely get it right. Holding a pick for a long time will most likely hurt at first, but you are going to get used to it in a few hours.

Lesson 3: Playing The Chords

Before moving on to the fretboard, it is important to familiarize yourself with the different guitar chords, so you can begin playing simple notes. A chord refers to a harmonic and balanced group of a minimum of three notes. To start, you need to know the two rudimentary types of chords: the first position chords, and the barre chords. Let us begin with the first.

Learning The 1st Position Chords

You can play the first position chords using a combination of pressed and open strings lying in the beginning three frets of your guitar. The common major chords are C Major, A Major, G Major, E Major, and D Major. Play them and you will become acquainted with them.

Now, practice shifting between these chords quickly. Write down different chord arrangements, play them, and then switch between these chord arrangements. This will help you understand the chords easily and quickly. Make sure to play the right notes. For instance, in A major, you do not strum the low E string. The notes not to be played will be marked with an 'X' on your guitar tablature.

Finger Placements For Different Chords

Next, you need to learn finger placements for different chords. You will play the major first and then the minor.

C Major: To play the C chord, position your ring finger right on the third fret of the second densest string. Place your middle finger right on the third thickest string's second fret and keep your index finger positioned on the second thinnest string's first fret. Strum and then play each of these strings individually while playing the C chord. Ensure every string rings out very clearly.

C major

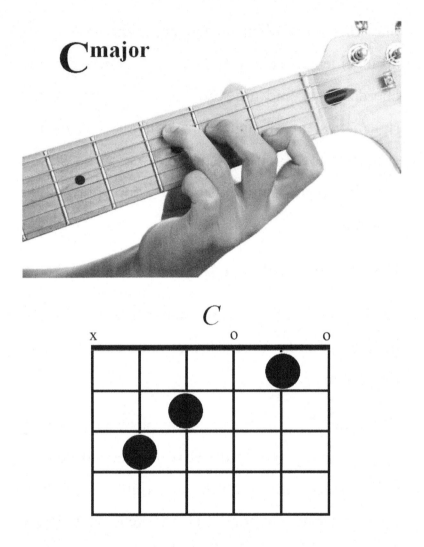

C

A Major: Use your ring, index, and middle fingers and place them right on the second fret of each of the second thinnest string, third thinnest string, and fourth thinnest string. Play each string, excluding the top-most one.

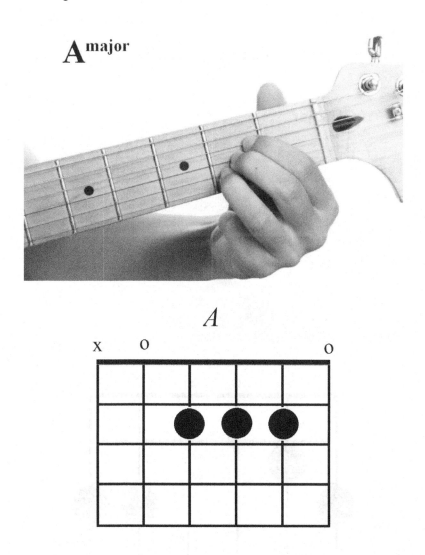

A **major**

A

G Major: To play the G chord, place your middle finger right on the thickest string's third fret. Place your index finger right on the second thickest string's second fret. Place the ring finger right on the thinnest string's third fret. Now strum, making sure every string rings out perfectly loud and clear.

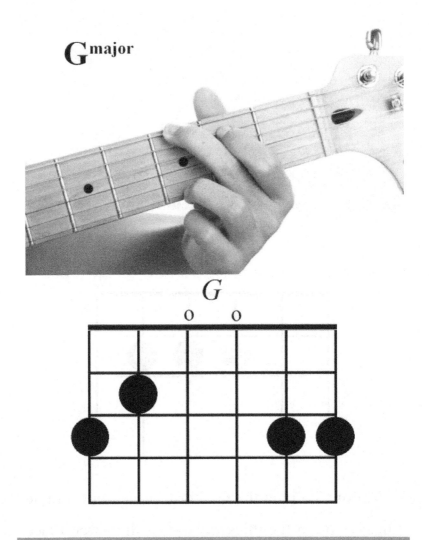

E Major: This is by far the easiest-to-play chord. Place your ring and middle fingers right on the second fret of the second densest string as well as the second fret of the third thickest string. Make sure the index finger is on the third thinnest string's first fret and play the chord.

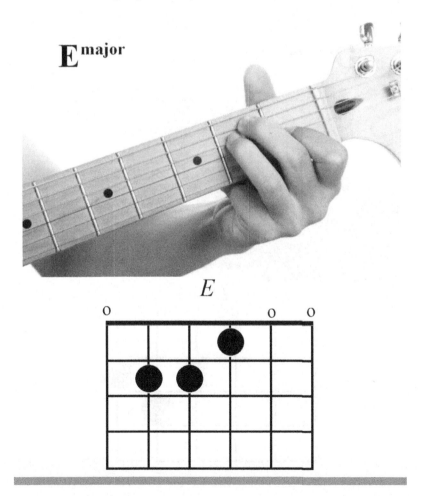

Tom Mahalo

D Major: To play the D major, place your index finger right on the second fret of the third slimmest string. Place the middle finger on the thinnest string's third fret, and your ring finger right on the third fret of the second slimmest string, play the bottom four strings and enjoy the sound.

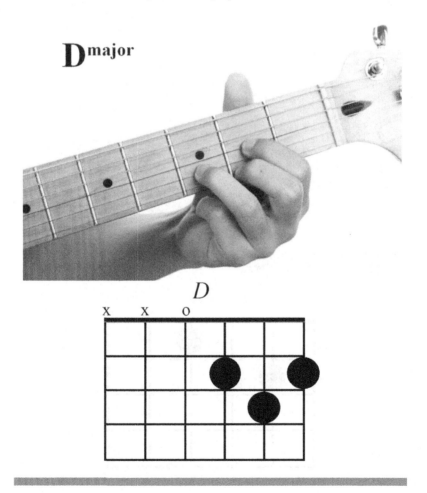

E Minor: This chord is incredibly similar to E major; however, in E minor, you do not make use of your index finger. Place your ring and middle fingers right on the second fret of the second thickest, as well as the second fret of the third densest strings and play it.

Em

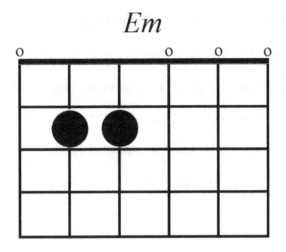

A Minor: Place your ring and middle fingers right on the third as well as the fourth densest strings' second frets. Your index finger should be on the second slimmest string's first fret. This chord has a shape quite similar to that of E major but is positioned one string below. Make sure to ignore the top string when playing A minor.

A^{minor}

Am

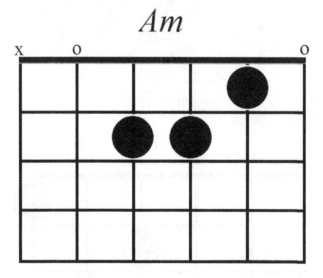

D Minor: D minor is quite similar to the D Major chord. To play the D minor, place your middle finger on the third slimmest string's second fret.

Place the index finger on the thinnest string's first fret and position the ring finger on the second slimmest string's third fret. Play the four bottom strings only.

Dm

Play all the chords repeatedly for at least two hours to become completely familiar with them.

How to get a crisp, clean sound

After learning the chords, practice playing them, so you can get a clean, crisp sound from each string in every chord. Play every string of the different chords, making sure every string that is supposed to ring in a chord does not mute or muffle.

If the notes do not ring out clearly, the likelihood is, you are not pressing the strings hard enough. It could also mean your fingers might be touching the string thus preventing the chords from having a clear sound. If you find any of your unused fingers touching any string, please keep them away from the strings not mentioned while using a chord. This will help you produce a clear sound.

Moreover, ensure your strumming/fretting fingers curl right above your fretboard when they touch the strings in such a manner that you are resting your fingers on an imaginary ball, or there is a marble tucked under the knuckle of every finger. This tactic ascertains there is enough space for all the open strings, so the chords ring out perfectly clear.

Strum in a relaxed, loose motion

While strumming the guitar, be careful of the motion you adopt. Strumming comprises of upstrokes and down-strokes in different combinations and demands you to strike every note of every chord rhythmically and evenly.

To ensure this happens, strum using a relaxed and loose motion. Make good use of your wrist to practice smooth downwards and upwards motions.

Your elbow should point towards the guitar and should be firmly in its place. Sweep your pick downwards on all the guitar strings and ensure your elbow does not move a lot and often because you execute strumming mostly from your wrist; therefore, if your elbow shifts positions frequently, your wrist will move as well, which will disturb the fluid motion of the strum. Keep this advice in mind, and you will be successful in strumming beautifully.

Learning The Barre Chords

The moveable or barre chords are incredibly helpful when it comes to playing a guitar. To play a barre chord, you use your index finger to strum or bar every note in one fret. For instance, to play an F (it is the movable chord in the first position), you need to barre every note on the very first fret using your index finger. You need to play in the shape of E chord but move one-step upwards on the neck using your index, little, and middle fingers.

Using this exact position of your fingers, press the second fret to produce the B chord. You will produce the G chord on the third fret. These positions are slightly difficult to learn; however, with constant practice, you will gain command of them.

Keep these lessons in mind and go over them repeatedly for about three hours until you master them. Once you grasp them, move to working your way on the guitar fretboard.

Lesson 4: Memorizing The Fretboard

Learning and memorizing the fretboard is perhaps the toughest part of guitar playing. However, once you learn a few tricks, navigating the fretboard like a pro becomes very simple. Before you take to cursing the fretboard several times, take a deep breath, and calm down.

Once calm, follow the steps described below and you will memorize the fretboard in a matter of hours.

The Chromatic Scale

The chromatic scale on a guitar is a sequence of 12 tones ascending or descending in increments of ½ step each (also known as one fret at one time). To simplify this, this scale gives names to every note on the guitar's neck in succession. There are two very simple rules you can use to memorize the guitar's chromatic scale.

First, understand that notes move in a sequence that begins on the C string and ends right on the B one and move in this manner C, D, E, F, G, A, and B. In between these notes, you will find sharps denoted by # and the flats denoted by b. A sharp gives a raise to a tone by just one fret, and one flat lowers a note by just one fret. However, there exist two exemptions to this particular rule. The note pairs E-F and B-C are only ½ step apart, which means there is no flat or sharp between them.

With the help of these two simple principles, you would arrive at this particular scale spelling:

C-C# |Db-D-D# |Eb-E-F-F# |Gb-G-G# |Ab-A-A# |Bb-B.

One thing that might change is going to be your starting pitch, as you can start the chromatic scale on any note.

The figure shown below is a comprehensive grid showing all the notes on the guitar's fretboard that end on the twelfth note. You will notice that the notes lying at the twelfth fret have a pitch similar to the open strings you had begun on; we refer to this as an 'octave'- notes at the same pitch, one registering higher. Right at this precise point, the scale will recycle itself upwards towards the neck. For instance, the thirteenth and the first notes have the same exact note names. When trying to inscribe the notes names onto your memory, use markers to assign names to different notes on your fretboard.

CHROMATIC SCALE ON ALL 6 STRINGS

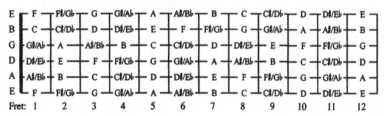

Move up and down the fretboard to memorize the chromatic scale. Going through this about four to five times will easily engrave the scale into your mind.

Horizontal Scale Patterns

After becoming acquainted with your guitar's chromatic scale, move to applying this knowledge to various different keys.

The figure shown below contains the names of notes in every minor and major key. The starting point on each line is the only difference between these two scales. For instance, C major begins on C and moves like C, D, E, F, G, A, B and the A minor key begins on A and moves like A, B, C, D, E, F, G.

SCALE TONES IN ALL 15 KEYS

KEY	SCALE TONES						
	1	2	3	4	5	6	7
C/Am	C	D	E	F	G	A	B
G/Em	G	A	B	C	D	E	F♯
D/Bm	D	E	F♯	G	A	B	C♯
A/F♯m	A	B	C♯	D	E	F♯	G♯
E/C♯m	E	F♯	G♯	A	B	C♯	D♯
B/G♯m	B	C♯	D♯	E	F♯	G♯	A♯
F♯/D♯m	F♯	G♯	A♯	B	C♯	D♯	E♯
C♯/A♯m	C♯	D♯	E♯	F♯	G♯	A♯	B♯
F/Dm	F	G	A	B♭	C	D	E
B♭/Gm	B♭	C	D	E♭	F	G	A
E♭/Cm	E♭	F	G	A♭	B♭	C	D
A♭/Fm	A♭	B♭	C	D♭	E♭	F	G
D♭/B♭m	D♭	E♭	F	G♭	A♭	B♭	C
G♭/E♭m	G♭	A♭	B♭	C♭	D♭	E♭	F
C♭/A♭m	C♭	D♭	E♭	F♭	G♭	A♭	B♭

Now you are aware of all the note names lying in every scale. Try exploring the guitar strings and fretboard and finding each string at a time. The figure below shows a two-bar phrase centered on the E major key. Over here, the open and high E string works as a pedaling tone between the tones of the other scales.

A two-bar phrase centered on the E major

The figure shown below is an exact replica of the figure above, but there is one thing differentiating the two. The figure below is entirely in E minor. Try finding the different notes in this key and keep strumming each string until you become acquainted with all the notes on the fretboard.

A great and fun tip to learn this easily is by recording your strumming. This way, you can listen to it repeatedly and recall each string. Practical application of the knowledge and information you have learned is a fantastic technique to memorize it.

A two-bar phrase centered on the E minor

Vertical Scale Patterns

After practicing the horizontal scale patterns, move on to working on the vertical scale ones. The figure shown below shows a G major scale in its third position. In this particular case, you are learning this scale across each of the six strings instead of playing one string at one time. To include the E high string, play notes A-B-C on the frets 5, 7 and 8 respectively.

G major scale in its third position

A huge benefit to the pattern-based scales is they are easily adjustable and movable. For example, if you use the pattern in the figure above, and shift this pattern up about two frets, you will get a major A scale. Try moving this pattern on the different areas of your guitar's neck and improvise all the keys you have learned previously. If you want to play it on any minor key, you can use the scale pattern shown in the image below.

This pattern can move to every minor key by just shifting the complete pattern to a dissimilar position on the guitar's neck. There are infinite possibilities when it comes to mixing the vertical and horizontal patterns, so put your imaginative cap on and explore the many avenues.

Learn The Octaves

Your next step is to learn the octaves. A great way to improve and speed up memorization of the fretboard is to locate every position on the guitar neck where a certain pitch can play well. The figure displayed below shows a set of frames showing different positions on the neck where the G note and its different octaves can be found.

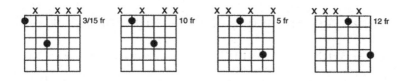

Practice different octaves on the G note to memorize them.

The figure below shows the G vertical major scale pattern you learned previously; but this time, it contains the octave of every scale tone.

Quite often, you will find that both the notes of one octave play simultaneously. This is a technique employed when using the guitar to play rock and jazz music. The figure below is an apt illustration of this very technique. Take a strum or a pick and use it with your thumb's side. Make sure to mute the string located right between the fretted notes using your finger's fleshy part.

After going through the aforementioned steps for five times, you will learn every note on each string and you will have realized that learning the fretboard was not as complicated as you initially thought.

Although, you will successfully learn most of it and will memorize enough of it to play your guitar by the end of the day, you should know that memorizing the guitar fretboard is an ongoing process. You need to go over these steps several times every day until they are engraved in your mind.

The figure below is the last image in this chapter; it shows you an eight-measure solo based in G major. This solo combines all the knowledge you have gained from this chapter and will help you understand what happens when everything comes together. Go ahead, try it, and then come up with something innovative of your own.

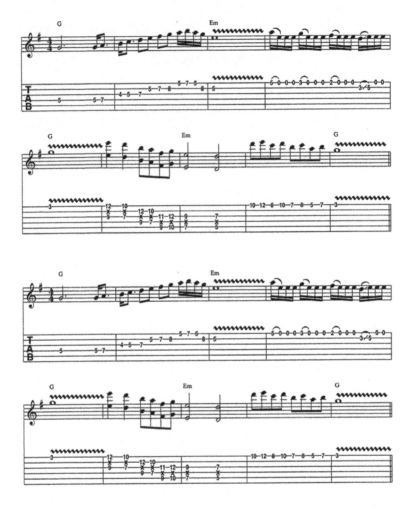

That was great, right? If you have successfully followed all these instructions outlined thus far to produce great music, then it is clear, you have what it takes to play the guitar. Keep moving and learn a few more things to complete your lesson.

Tom Mahalo

Lesson 5: Reading The Tablature And Practicing Basic Songs

Well done for making it thus far, clearly, your passion in the guitar and learning how to play it is undying; further, thus far, you have done a great job.

Now, you need to learn how to read the guitar tablature, practice some basic songs, and get used to bearing the slight pain you experience from holding the guitar and strumming with the pick, and you will be done for the day.

Let us begin our last lesson of how to play guitar in just one day.

Reading The Guitar Tablature

Guitarists have a specific system of musical notes and notation known as the guitar tablature commonly referred to as the guitar tab. When you have a tablature corresponding to a certain musical piece, look at every line positioned in the 'staff' part of the tablature just the way you look at the guitar. Every line corresponds to one particular string and every number on the line helps you know which fret you need to press down while plucking that particular string.

For instance, to play the note shown below from 'Sweet Home Alabama', play only two notes on open D string, making sure the B string is at the third fret, with the G lying at the second fret.

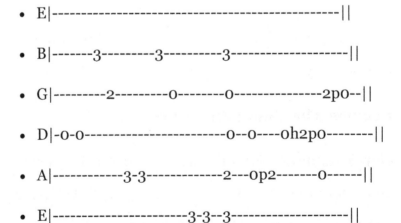

- E|--||

- B|-------3---------3----------3-------------------||

- G|---------2---------0--------0--------------2po--||

- D|-o-o---------------------o--o----oh2po--------||

- A|------------3-3-------------2---0p2-------0-----||

- E|----------------------3-3--3-------------------||

If you switch between chords and licks, you will feel like you are actually making some good music. Use the guitar tablature of different songs and keep all the information you have learned previously to try your hand at some simple songs.

Managing Finger Pain

Managing your finger pain is another thing you need to take care of in the start. After playing the guitar and strumming on it for a couple of hours, your fingers will be sore. Your fingers will experience a searing pain that seems hard to bear, remember, this is normal and something every guitarist goes through in the start. Focus on your passion and goal and use it to build enough strength inside you to withstand this pain.

Moreover, you also need to take care of your fingers from the very first day, so you can prevent the pain from getting worse and soothe your fingers. For that, you need to keep a box of ice and a container full of apple cider vinegar near you each time you play your acoustic. Put ice on your sore fingers or soak them in the vinegar to reduce the pain you are experiencing.

You can also dip your fingers in a little rubbing alcohol. This speeds up the process of callus build-up. When callous builds up, your fingers become strong enough to strum the strings easily, and you do not experience much pain. Make sure you do not dip them in the rubbing alcohol before you play the guitar because this can interfere with smooth playing of the guitar.

Final Tips

Here are some final tips that will help you play the guitar easily and overcome the difficulties you experience in the initial few hours.

1. 1. If a certain chord does not ring out clearly and as it should, play every string in that chord to find out whether you are muting a certain string, or are playing a chord the wrong way. This helps you attack the problematic areas of that chord and easily rectify them. Ensure to use the tips of your fingers to build the chord as this will make the strings sound clearer and brighter.

2. Please do not become frustrated if the chords do not sound good at first. This is the very first time you are playing a guitar; it is highly unlikely you can strum the strings firmly and with enough strength in the very beginning. Keep working at it and keep strumming. Gradually, your fingers will get sufficient strength to press on every string firmly and in the correct manner.

3. Making mistakes is normal; do not be harsh on yourself when you err. Instead, appreciate your efforts and treat yourself to a little break or something delicious after completing each lesson given in this guide.

4. If fretting is extremely challenging for you, use a lighter string. They will not sound as good as the hard ones, but they are easier to strum and will cause far less pain in the fingers as well. This is a very good beginner's tip.

5. Use a pick to pluck the strong and thick strings so you can save your fingers from becoming incredibly sore.

6. Print the chord and fretboard diagrams shown in this book and hang them at a place you come across all the time. This will help you go over them repeatedly, which will engrain them in your mind.

7. Practice playing your guitar with a friend or two who share the same passion, or who are learning to play any other musical instrument. This helps you understand that everyone goes through a rough patch in the start. Moreover, your guitar sessions will become fun with the addition of a friend and this will help you feel more relaxed.

Follow these tips and pay heed to all the guidance given in this guitar-playing guide. If you stick to it, you will most certainly be able to play a basic song on your guitar and impress your family members by the end of the day.

!!!BONUS!!! PICTURES OF CHORDS, 5 FAMOUS SONGS TO PLAY WITHIN 24 HOURS

Playing Simple Songs

Around 90 percent of all guitar-based music is just composed of three to four chords; therefore, playing any song is not difficult at all. Playing a specific song might seem daunting at first, but if you read its tablature and calm down, you will slowly be able to play it very well. Here are a few basic, simple guitar chord songs that are perfect for novices.

- Knockin´ on Heaven´s Door - Bob Dylan Chords
- Hand in My Pocket - Alanis Morissette Chords
- The One I Love - REM Chords
- What´s Up - For Non-Blondes Chords

- Stay with Me - Sam Smith Chords
- Something in the Way - Nirvana
- Last Kiss - Pearl Jam
- Chasing Cars - Snow Patrol
- As the Tears Go - the Rolling Stones
- Hey Soul Sister - Train

Try any one or two songs you like best or find the easiest one. You can easily find their tablatures online. Get their printout and use it to play a song's chords. Practice a song at least five times so you the hang of it and can play it without any difficulty. Once you can play it effortlessly, move to another song. Try working on one song every day and slowly make a collection of songs you can play beautifully. I believe in you! You can do it! Trust in yourself! Don't wait and practice, practice, practice! Good luck!

Knockin´ on heaven´s door - Bob Dylan

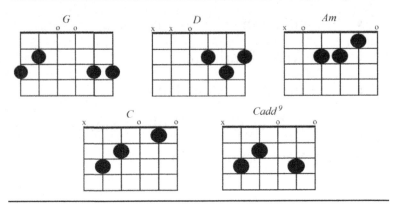

GDAm
Mama take this badge off of me
GDC
I can't use it any-more
GDAm
It's getting dark, too dark for me to see
GDC
I feel I'm knockin on heaven's door

GDAm
Knock, knock, knockin' on heaven's door
GDC
Knock, knock, knockin' on heaven's door
GDAm
Knock, knock, knockin' on heaven's door
GDC
Knock, knock, knockin' on heaven's door

The one i love - REM

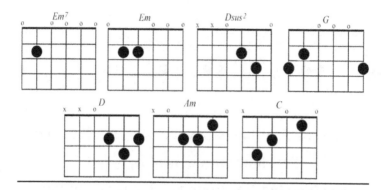

EmDsus2EmEm7
This one goes out to the one I love
EmDsus2EmEm7
This one goes out to the one I've left behind
GDAmC
A simple prop to occupy my time
EmDsus2EmEm7
This one goes out to the one I love
EmDsus2EmEm7
This one goes out to the one I love
EmDsus2EmEm7
This one goes out to the one I've left behind
GDAmC
Another prop has occupied my time
EmDsus2EmEm7
This one goes out to the one I love
EmDsus2EmEm7
Fire (she's comin' down on her own, now)
EmDsus2EmEm7
Fire (she's comin' down on her own, now)

Hand in my pocket - Alanis Morissette

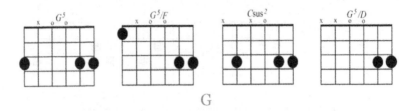

G

I'm broke but I'm happy, I'm sore but I'm kind

I'm short but I'm healthy, yeah

I'm high but I'm grounded, I'm sane but I'm

overwhelmed

I'm lost but I'm hopeful, baby

Chorus:

F

And what it all comes down to

CG

Is that everything's gonna be fine, fine, fine

F

Cause I got one hand in my pocket

CC9G

And the other one is givin' a high five

Stay with me - Sam Smith

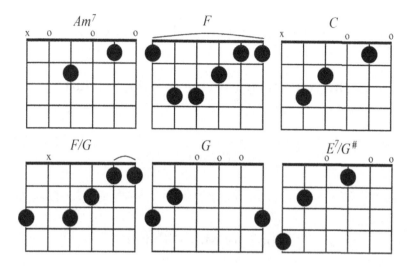

AmFC

Won't you stay with me?

AmFC

Cause you're all I need

GAmFC

This ain't love it's clear to see

G#dimAmFC

But darling, stay with me

Am7FC

Why am I so emotional?

Am7FC

No it's not a good look, gain some self control

Am7FC

And deep down I know this never works

Am7G5/FC

But you can lay with me so it doesn't hurt

[Chorus]

AmFC

Won't you stay with me?

AmFC

Cause you're all I need

GAmFC

This ain't love it's clear to see

G#dimAmFC

But darling, stay with me

What´s up - 4 non blonde

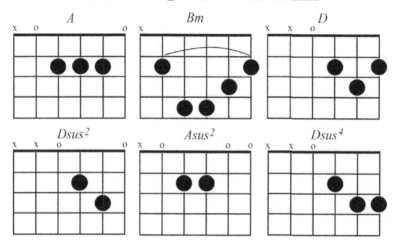

G
And I said Heyeyeyeyey
Am
Heyeyey
CG
I said Hey Whats going on?
G
And I said Heyeyeyeyey
Am
Heyeyey
CG
I said Hey Whats going on?

GAmCG
Ooh, Ooh Ooh
GAm
And I try, oh my god do I try

Tom Mahalo

CG
I try all the time, in this institution
GAm
And I pray, oh my god do I pray
C
I pray every single day
G
For a revolution

Tom Mahalo

Something in the Way - Nirvana

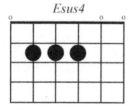

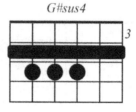

G#sus4   Esus4

Underneath the bridge

G#sus4   Esus4

The tarp has sprung a leak

G#sus4   Esus4

And the animals I've trapped

G#sus4   Esus4

Have all become my pets

G#sus4   Esus4

And I'm living off of grass

G#sus4   Esus4

And the drippings from the ceiling

G#sus4   Esus4

It's okay to eat fish

G#sus4   Esus4

'Cause they don't have any feelings

Tom Mahalo

Last Kiss - Pearl Jam

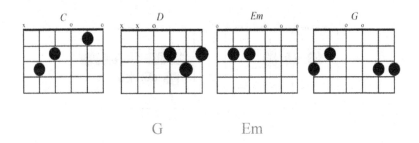

         G   Em

Oh, where oh where can my baby be

         C   D

The Lord took her away from me

    G   Em

She's gone to heaven so I've got to be good

     C   D   G

So I can see my baby when I leave ... this world

Tom Mahalo

Chasing Cars - Snow Patrol

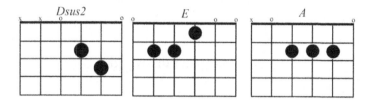

A

We'll do it all

E

Everything

Dsus2

On our own

A

We don't need

E

Anything

Dsus2

Or anyone

A

If I lay here

E

If I just lay here

Dsus2

Would you lie with me

A

And just forget the world?

Tom Mahalo

As the Tears Go - the Rolling Stones

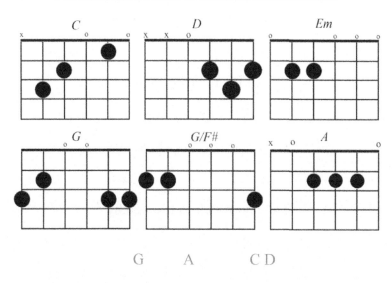

<pre>
        G   A   C D
</pre>

It is the evening of the day

<pre>
        G   A   C D
</pre>

I sit and watch the children play

<pre>
                C   D
</pre>

Smiling faces I can see

<pre>
            G - G/F# - Em
</pre>

But not for me

<pre>
        C   C   D D
</pre>

I sit and watch as tears go by

<pre>
        G   A   C D
</pre>

My richness can't buy everything

Tom Mahalo

G A   C D

I want to hear to children sing

    C   D

All I here is the sound

   G - G/F# - Em

Of rain falling on the ground

  C   C   D D

I sit and watch as tears go by

Hey Soul Sister - Train

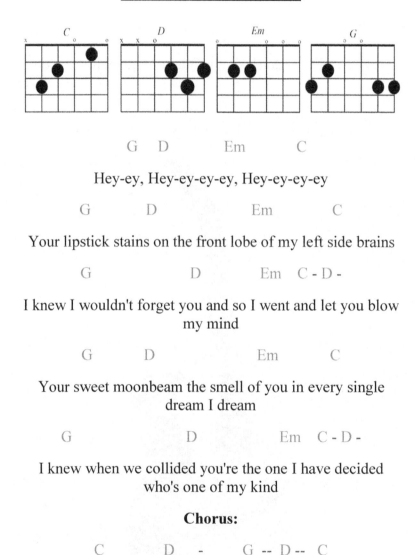

G   D   Em   C

Hey-ey, Hey-ey-ey-ey, Hey-ey-ey-ey

G   D   Em   C

Your lipstick stains on the front lobe of my left side brains

G   D   Em   C - D -

I knew I wouldn't forget you and so I went and let you blow
my mind

G   D   Em   C

Your sweet moonbeam the smell of you in every single
dream I dream

G   D   Em   C - D -

I knew when we collided you're the one I have decided
who's one of my kind

Chorus:

C   D   -   G -- D -- C

Hey soul sister ain't that mister mister on the radio stereo

Tom Mahalo

D - G -- D --

The way you move ain't fair you know

C   D   -   G -- D -- C   D

Hey soul sister I don't want to miss a single thing you do

G   D   Em   C

Tonight Hey-ey, Hey-ey-ey-ey, Hey-ey-ey-ey

Tom Mahalo

Helpful Tips To Practice Basic Chords

To play these chords successfully and master them in a matter of days, you can use the following tips:

Bend all your knuckles because it helps you form the 'claw' hand as discussed earlier.

Make sure when you press the strings, you use your fingertips and not the whole pad of your finger.

When pressing a string, ensure your finger is not pressing the string above or below it as well.

Your finger should be as close to the fret as possible.

Be sure to place your thumb behind the neck of your guitar and not on top of it.

Master each chord by playing it several times a day.

Once you master all the cords, combine them, and switch between them. Start with a combination of three chords first and then move on to four chords.

Give your fingers rest and do not overdo it.

Exercising these tips helps you play the chords easily and perfect them.

In the next bit of our learning, we will learn how to memorize the fretboard.

<u>Conclusion</u>

As this book has clearly shown you, learning how to play a guitar is not difficult or complex. It simply requires passion and a good guide. This book fulfills the second condition. Now, you just need to ignite your guitar playing passion and you will be on your way to mastering the art of playing your acoustic or electric guitar.

Thank you again for purchasing this book!

I hope this book was able to help you to teach you how to play a guitar in the shortest time possible.

Tom Mahalo

The next step is to practice and practice some more until you become great at playing the guitar.

Thank you and good luck!

Tom Mahalo

Made in the USA
Las Vegas, NV
04 February 2024

85262721R00046